Shining
Stars

Shining Stars

Bahá'í Prayers and Passages for Children

BELLWOOD
PRESS®

EVANSTON, ILLINOIS

Bellwood Press
1233 Central St., Evanston, IL 60202

Printed in the United States of America
on acid-free paper ∞

ISBN: 978-1-61851-272-7
28 27 26 25   4 3 2 1

Illustrations and book and cover design
by Kathryn Adebayo

The prayers and passages compiled in this book
follow the order in which they appear in the
grades 2 and 3 branch courses of the
Ruhi Book 3 children's class materials.

Prayers

From Children's Classes: Grade Two

O Lord! I am a child; enable me to grow beneath the shadow of Thy loving-kindness. I am a tender plant; cause me to be nurtured through the outpourings of the clouds of Thy bounty. I am a sapling of the garden of love; make me into a fruitful tree.

Thou art the Mighty and the Powerful, and Thou art the All-Loving, the All-Knowing, the All-Seeing.

~'Abdu'l-Bahá

O my God! O my God! Unite the hearts of Thy servants, and reveal to them Thy great purpose. May they follow Thy commandments and abide in Thy law. Help them, O God, in their endeavor, and grant them strength to serve Thee. O God! Leave them not to themselves, but guide their steps by the light of Thy knowledge, and cheer their hearts by Thy love. Verily, Thou art their Helper and their Lord.

~Bahá'u'lláh

O my God! O my God! Thou seest these children who are the twigs of the tree of life, the birds of the meads of salvation, the pearls of the ocean of Thy grace, the roses of the garden of Thy guidance.

O God, our Lord! We sing Thy praise, bear witness to Thy sanctity and implore fervently the heaven of Thy mercy to make us lights of guidance, stars shining above the horizons of eternal glory amongst mankind, and to teach us a knowledge which proceedeth from Thee. Yá Bahá'u'l-Abhá!

~'Abdu'l-Bahá

Passages from the Bahá'í Writings

From Children's Classes: Grade Two

Intone, O My servant, the verses of God that have been received by thee, as intoned by them who have drawn nigh unto Him, that the sweetness of thy melody may kindle thine own soul, and attract the hearts of all men.

~Bahá'u'lláh

It is the greatest longing of every soul who is attracted to the Kingdom of God to find time to turn with entire devotion to his Beloved, so as to seek His bounty and blessing and immerse himself in the ocean of communion, entreaty and supplication.

~'Abdu'l-Bahá

O Son of Light! Forget all save Me and commune with My spirit. This is of the essence of My command, therefore turn unto it.

~Bahá'u'lláh

O Son of Being! My love is My stronghold; he that entereth therein is safe and secure, and he that turneth away shall surely stray and perish.

~Bahá'u'lláh

The Tongue of My power hath, from the heaven of My omnipotent glory, addressed to My creation these words: "Observe My commandments, for the love of My beauty."

~Bahá'u'lláh

Know assuredly that My commandments are the lamps of My loving providence among My servants, and the keys of My mercy for My creatures.

~Bahá'u'lláh

The purpose of God in creating man hath been, and will ever be, to enable him to know his Creator and to attain His Presence.

~Bahá'u'lláh

Exert every effort to acquire the various branches of knowledge and true understanding. Strain every nerve to achieve both material and spiritual accomplishments.

~'Abdu'l-Bahá

He must search after the truth to the utmost of his ability and exertion, that God may guide him in the paths of His favor and the ways of His mercy.

~Bahá'u'lláh

Prayers

From Children's Classes: Grade Three

O Lord God! Make us as waves of the sea, as flowers of the garden, united, agreed through the bounties of Thy love. O Lord! Dilate the breasts through the signs of Thy oneness, and make all mankind as stars shining from the same height of glory, as perfect fruits growing upon Thy tree of life.

Verily, Thou art the Almighty, the Self-Subsistent, the Giver, the Forgiving, the Pardoner, the Omniscient, the One Creator.

~'Abdu'l-Bahá

O my Lord! Make Thy beauty to be my food, and Thy presence my drink, and Thy pleasure my hope, and praise of Thee my action, and remembrance of Thee my companion, and the power of Thy sovereignty my succorer, and Thy habitation my home, and my dwelling-place the seat Thou hast sanctified from the limitations imposed upon them who are shut out as by a veil from Thee.

Thou art, verily, the Almighty, the All-Glorious, the Most Powerful.

~Bahá'u'lláh

O Lord! Unto Thee I repair for refuge, and toward all Thy signs I set my heart.

O Lord! Whether traveling or at home, and in my occupation or in my work, I place my whole trust in Thee.

Grant me then Thy sufficing help so as to make me independent of all things, O Thou Who art unsurpassed in Thy mercy!

Bestow upon me my portion, O Lord, as Thou pleasest, and cause me to be satisfied with whatsoever Thou hast ordained for me.

Thine is the absolute authority to command.

~The Báb

O Thou kind Lord! These lovely children are the handiwork of the fingers of Thy might and the wondrous signs of Thy greatness. O God! Protect these children, graciously assist them to be educated and enable them to render service to the world of humanity. O God! These children are pearls, cause them to be nurtured within the shell of Thy loving-kindness.

Thou art the Bountiful, the All-Loving.

~'Abdu'l-Bahá

Passages from the Bahá'í Writings

From Children's Classes: Grade Three

So powerful is the light of unity that it can illuminate the whole earth.

~*Bahá'u'lláh*

We ask God to endow human souls with justice so that they may be fair, and may strive to provide for the comfort of all . . .

~*'Abdu'l-Bahá*

The supreme need of humanity is cooperation and reciprocity.

~ *'Abdu'l-Bahá*

have created thee rich and have bountifully shed My favor upon thee.

~Bahá'u'lláh

admonish you to observe courtesy, for above all else it is the prince of virtues. Well is it with him who is illumined with the light of courtesy and is attired with the vesture of uprightness.

~Bahá'u'lláh

They must endeavor to consort in a friendly spirit with everyone, must follow moderation in their conduct, must have respect and consideration one for another and show loving-kindness and tender regard to all the peoples of the world.

~ 'Abdu'l-Bahá

Incline your hearts, O people of God, unto the counsels of your true, your incomparable Friend.

~Bahá'u'lláh

O ye beloved of the Lord! Commit not that which defileth the limpid stream of love or destroyeth the sweet fragrance of friendship.

~Bahá'u'lláh

Strive ye with all your might to create, through the power of the Word of God, genuine love, spiritual communion and durable bonds among individuals.

~ *'Abdu'l-Bahá*

That one indeed is a man who, today, dedicateth himself to the service of the entire human race.

~Bahá'u'lláh

Waste not your time in idleness and sloth. Occupy yourselves with that which profiteth yourselves and others.

~Bahá'u'lláh

It is incumbent upon each one of you to engage in some occupation—such as a craft, a trade or the like. We have exalted your engagement in such work to the rank of worship of the one true God.

~Bahá'u'lláh